THOUGHT CATALOG BOOKS

Being Human

Being Human

JULIA GARI WEISS

Thought Catalog Books

Brooklyn, NY

THOUGHT CATALOG BOOKS

Copyright © 2016 by Julia Gari Weiss

All rights reserved. Published by Thought Catalog Books, a division of The Thought & Expression Co., Williamsburg, Brooklyn. Founded in 2010, Thought Catalog is a website and imprint dedicated to your ideas and stories. We publish fiction and non-fiction from emerging and established writers across all genres. For general information and submissions: manuscripts@thoughtcatalog.com.

First edition, 2016

ISBN 978-0692722534

10 9 8 7 6 5 4 3 2 1

Cover Image © Henn Kim / Offset.com, Cover Design © KJ Parish

DEDICATION

This is for Harold Gross, Janet Gross, David Weiss, Laura Gross Weiss, Ellen Trujillo, Erika Weiss, Frank Moczulewski, Jeffrey Peterson, and Chris Antzoulis.

I am grateful every day for Gisella DeMorais, Leslie Anderson, Daniel Gould, Marissa Frykman, Carolyn Kelton, Pat Pallasche, Danielle and Jerrel Burgo, Anna DeRuyter, Kovie and Ejus Biakolo, Burton and Ruth Weiss, Keith Abate, Tami Walsh, Justin Meron Smith, Ahmir Thompson, Tariq Trotter, John Paul White, Joy Williams, Bobby Bones, the Shields family, and the Greene family. Thank you for making me a better human.

ACKNOWLEDGEMENTS

"Toast" is for Janet Gross
"Malignant Neoplasm" is for Ellen Trujillo and Janet Gross
"Exhibition Game" is for Harold Gross, in his honor
"Being Human" is for David Weiss and Gail Johnson
"Such A Lovely Place (Such A Lovely Place)" is for Laura Weiss
"Again" is for Laura Weiss
"Heavy Lifting" is for Erika Weiss

APPRECIATION

Thank you to my mentors, Kevin Pilkington, Kate Knapp Johnson, and Vijay Seshadri for shaping my work, both physically and metaphorically.

Contents

DEDICATED TO YOU,
FOR WE
HAVE ALL FELT THE
TEAR AND TRIUMPH
THE
THRILL AND THROBBING
OF
BEING HUMAN.

"BE KIND,
FOR EVERYONE YOU MEET IS FIGHTING
A HARD BATTLE"

Ghosts

The tracks are rattling, buzzing
alive. We are tapping our fingers,
checking wristwatches for departure time,
though we have a schedule in hand,
which details every minute –
when we board with our black briefcases
or beige high heels or wool overcoats –
knowing each routine stop from memory
and no idea where we're headed.

Lulled to sleep through most
of the ride, waking only to hand our ticket
to a conductor who doesn't look
anyone in the eyes so we assume
s/he's the same person every day.

I haven't been on board lately.
Got lost visiting stations,
counting passing faces, examining maps,
reading overhead signs again and again –
trying to remember getting off here.
Footsteps check traffic reports
with no alternative route,
check weather with no umbrellas,
and buy an unlimited ticket to a destination
written in invisible ink.

Aperture

There is a steel door,
it's heavy, requires my feet
firmly planted, body shifted,
I must tug with my biceps,
abdominals, squinted eyes,
clamp my jaw. With all that force
it may budge, open a crack.

There are more doors:
oak, redwood, chiffon, plastic,
all lined up in front of me.
The paper door is weightless,
easier to pull. Shows me dirt –
not as spectacular as what's behind
the barbed wire door, I'm sure,
I wouldn't know, never opened it before.
Time is lined with walls of doors.
The more trying, the more triumphant.
I hang on to handles, hoist one open,
a gust of wind scintillating my skin.

For that brief moment, I know why
there are doors in rows, why
I build myself up to open okra,
and why I touch handles to try
and pry open particular doors,
while others are better left closed.

Again

We thought Cancer left
he went on vacation,
now he's back on our doorstep
with a bullshit Hawaiian shirt and suitcases
to begin unpacking the baggage
we thought we'd kept hidden
and take the few cells left in her.

I keep saying "it's fine"
but thinking "it's final."
I replay the dripping IVs, dry heaves,
and time keeps slowly circling
when it should be yielding.

I can't stop double-checking the door –
I swear I locked it. I swear I did before.
My mother says, "it's okay." She says,
"Julia. Just let him in.
Or he'll break the lock,
smash the hinge,
destroy our entire foundation.
He wasn't that bad when he first visited.
I still have the wigs
and the will to live.
It's okay." She says, again and again.
"It's okay.
Let him in."

Sick of Sorry

Saying "I'm sorry" doesn't move veins
to pulsate. I'm sorry saying "I'm sorry" seems reductive,
simple English terms don't have the tenderness
of touch. I'm sorry "love" is the only
word to describe thirty five years of promise. Really,
I'm sorry. For your loss,
for these small sentences
that struggle to envelop
significance. You said "until death"
he lies still in a coffin. I'm sorry.
There isn't text for this ache
resounding thru my ribs.
I'd love to pry them open, show you,
since the universe has limited us to words,
to this constraint language, where we show up in black
attire, say "I'm sorry", hug, expect idioms to be enough.
"I'm sorry" is not a defibrillator. You warrant movement.
I enclosed you too tight, too long, did you feel it?
I made you make eye contact with me, did you see?
I was infiltrating my sentiments. Feel this. I'm sorry.
I was hoping you spoke body. This restrictive dialect
cannot express in five letters or less
my distress. I held you close to try and hold you
together. My heart pumping against yours
to hammer in persuasion,
to beat bereavement in,
wanting to resonate its throbbing apology. I'm sorry
to offer you words, only this.
You deserve more than I can give.

Black & Blue

We all dressed in black, except for the Marines
and you, who wore dress blues,
gold medallions, and the initials they stitched,
which felt like purloined letters,
etched afterthoughts for the afterlife.

Stars and stripes wrapped around your casket like a blanket statement.
How many times did the priest rehearse that exhaustive speech?
Welcoming us to this "premature burial" felt insincere postmortem.
Saying you "will be missed" made me wonder why the bullet hadn't.
You were "a good man" doesn't describe how you taught me to wash
windows or flashed your .44 caliber anytime a boy went near me,
nor did it conjure the O rings you created with La Flor Domicanas
like tiny floating clouds from the heaven where he's saying you reside.

I imagined you sitting in the pews, saying, "Who the fuck invited him?"
Which forced me to smile for the first time since seeing that serious oval
portrait the photographer tried to upsell me on, like the florist who told
me for "only extra 9.99," I could get "mo' roses" in red, white, and blue;
I swear how she said it, in her Asian accent, it sounded like "morose."

I know it was worth it to you, Keith,
but wonder if you witnessed the scene:
The men in blue carrying you thru this mass of black,
watching you being lowered into U.S. land and encasing you,
a misshapen bruise staring into a six foot hole,
rubbing dirt into a wound that will never heal.

Learning

Anna is trying to hand my
favor back. Raised six blocks away,
given this awkwardness, this guilt
of never taking. Never supplied
brand new books like private school kids.
Ours gave us torn copies, but we were lucky –
we had what we had –
though we eventually returned it.
Never kept what we didn't
buy or earn. We're learning.

I edited her essay, she wrote me
a thank-you letter, and now she's
displaying her party tricks for payback,
saying, "Pick." I say, *this is what friends are for*.
We sit in her living room, play board games,
and never get bored. We philosophize, whine,
pour wine. We reflect on old choices,
exchange nuisances, without expecting
anything in return. This is what friends are for.
We're learning.

On Our Deathbed

When you are 93
breathing in a ventilator beside me
I will still say to you
what I said at 33:
"You took too damn long."

Maybe you'll say, "60 years!"
And I'll say, "We could've had 63."
Your smile lines will stretch
while I think about 27, when I sat
wondering if you needed a match
to see the roadmap in pitch-black.

There were no streetlights
on Flatbush at midnight
when I determined to become moonlight
to live like a wild flare blazing on
so you'd notice the flicker of flames
guiding you home.

Armor

They are standing face to face
a foot away from one another
backs to the wall
in the narrow back entrance hall.
I tip toe between them,
wishing for invisibility.
There are no words exchanged
trailing behind me towards the elevator.
I push the button, the three of us wait.
He is definitely going up. She has a black duffel bag,
seems unsure whether to carry it up or away.
He stands, heavyset, black beard, white tank, board shorts.
She is petite in pink and white striped pajamas,
a tan oversized coat, charcoal hair pulled back,
eyes sullen under white rimmed glasses.
We all shuffle in; I push 10, say what floor?
He says 8, walks in, turns around, eyes intent,
watching numbers pass above the doors.
She gets in, insists on facing him, toe to toe.
She watches – her eyes by his lips – waiting
for recognition or guilt, a hint.
He's still intent on the floors above the doors,
one by one, they stand this way, facing, blaming, 3, 4.
She says que?
And he says mi amor!
Not mi amor: my love, my dear,
but mi amor: I'm tired, exhausted,
do we have to do this again?
She's still gazing into his eyes at 8.
He's peering above, not budging.
The doors open, they get out,
her walking backwards to the left,
him turning to me, "have a good night."
Then following her, sluggishly.

Cocaine & Colors

Cocaine Natalie
snorts off her key
in Geometry tells me
we see colors distinctly.

Like, your purple may be
what I see as green.
May see this as red
but I see blue jean.

So I look at the board
see shapes and angles
ask, is my circle the same
as your obtuse triangle?

No, because we create shapes
says Natalie, unlike the colors
they are learned perceptions
can't be confused with each other,

see, contours are concise
they are something we draw
in any hue ink color
big is vast and tiny is small.

She opens the baggy
inserts her house key,
says this may be orange to you
but it's white to me.

We see uniform colors
though call them different names
while we're both still right
since the shade is the same.

I nod thinking Natalie
might be on to something, like
you may hate black
but that could be my white.

—

The Weight

I was hollow shadows holding
onto four hours of sleep
and Ambien, wearing
sunglasses inside, under
excruciatingly dim lights.
My eye sockets sinking
into my cheekbones. People
would visit my mom's
hospital room with omelets
that I couldn't stomach. I'd cling
to coffee watching her
debilitating body, shrinking.
Visitors told me I looked thin,
wonderful even, and what
had I been doing lately?
I'd say, "starving."
Marvelous!
"Popping melatonin."
Fabulous!
"Sipping saltwater
pouring down my cheeks."
You. Look. Stunning!

When I reverted back
to myself over time,
healing, becoming fleshy
again, nobody said
a word. And I can't
recall seeing my reflection
in straight lines and baggy
blue jeans and feeling sexy.
Nor do I remember
this inept vanity in society
to treat sizable people

as invisible
until they're molded
to shrink to exist, inch by inch,
to become smaller and smaller,
until they show their clavicle.
That's when you finally notice them:
when they're disappearing altogether.

Appointment

They are full today.
It is a blocked date.
We are dying to get in,
everyone is dying;
there is no room for death
with nurses on vacation,
so you'll have to wait
for a space in your name.
Hold that pain, drink
your pills, take all the mgs,
and they'll be with you, shortly.

My mother holds her bowel
movements and platelets
in one hand, gesturing
with the other. In her agony,
she says, "It's terrible that
they're full. Really terrible
that all those rooms are filled."

Clumps

My mother shrieks in the shower.
I look up, see her holding
a chunk of reddish-brown hair.
She gets out, dries,
dresses, and now
it's everywhere – in the drain,
on her sweater, a portion on her
shoulder. When she's distracted
I remove stray strands so she doesn't
notice. Some stick in the wig she tries.
When she combs her hair
a clump stays lifeless in the brush.
She stares at it, frightened, and says,
"Do you think that's from me?" And I say,
"No, probably the person before us."

Carboplatin

In green "350."
In orange "IVF + ADDITIVES."
It flashes on an alaris monitor
sideways to the left.
Every time it disappears
it comes back again.

My mother's asleep in the hospital bed.
She wakes to say, "that movie is supposed to be good."
Falls asleep again.
Minutes later, "We should see that tonight."
All that's playing scrolls across the screen.
I want to turn the IV to show her
but she wakes again, "I had a dream about tigers."
I nod.
"ADDITIVES" scrolls across the screen in orange again.
And "350" in neon green

never goes away.

Not in the Pamphlets

The pamphlets don't mention that when she tells you,
you will lose feeling in your legs, you will fall
to the floor, scream, *No, no, no, please, no, no!*
Or that you will imagine her in a coffin, already dead, that the doctor
will tell you stage three, colon and ovarian.
The doctor will say *four-hour surgery,*
just to keep you on your toes, your heart in your throat
for an extra three hours or so. That the doctor will come into
the waiting room, mention invisible cells nobody
can see, say *necessary,* say *chemotherapy.*

The doctor won't add that she'll wake up
and her hair will fall out, like that.
It doesn't happen gradually,
or in a given time period. She'll wake up
this morning, and her hair sheds in clumps.
When you go wig shopping, chunks of her dark hair
stay in the wig. In her hairbrush. Stray
in clusters: on the floor, sweaters, rug,
in her laundry, drain, pillowcase.

A patient in chemo room six says *Latisse works.*
She will paint it on her left and right eyelid
where her eyelashes used to be, she paints
her left and right eyebrow, that she now
pencils in when she leaves the house. She will
squirt little dabs on brushes and paint them again
every night, hoping they grow back quickly.
She has cancelled all the hair appointments
she made a year in advance. She won't need them.
There is no hair on her legs, a few strands on her head.
A woman at Floyd's Barbers will try and charge $30
for seven snips. Your mother will show her her almost
baldness, and the barber says *if you don't like our price you*

don't have to get your cut here. You will try to strangle
this woman but mom will not let you. She says, *it's okay.*
Even when it's certainly not okay. None of this is okay.
Her best friend, a survivor will say, *do you still
have your pubic hair? I lost everything but my pubic
hair! I mean, what a bitch! The only hair you'd be fine
with losing is still hanging on for dear life!* And they'll laugh
and laugh, and cry and cry, and hold each other, and sob.

There won't be enough arms to hold you up
when your friends disappear. They don't know how to be here,
there is no right thing to say. No magical departure.
Some of her friends will send flowers, call,
ask her how she's doing. Some will do nothing at all.
The most beautiful thing about this are the ones who
do more than come through. Who show up at eight when you said
noon. Who hold her hand when she's snoring. Who sleepover
but never fall asleep. Help change her sheets
when the muscle relaxants don't warn her she needs to pee.
This is when friends become family, others fade entirely.

There is no preparation for the time commitment.
They'll write four hours on your schedule, this will be
ridiculously funny. It's a 12-hour spree, six at the least.
You'll be here with her every day: chemo days one, two.
Hydration days three, four, five.
Bandage change every week. Break six, seven.
Chemo eight. Doctor's appointment the following week.
Repeat. She'll throw up on two, three, four
most likely. She won't be able to sleep. She won't
eat. Everything will taste metallic, even water.
You'll know every nurse on staff by their first names:
Wes, Gail, Jin-Wong, Zara, Erin, Cyndy, Mary, Raquel,
Deborah, Casey, Anita, Ronald. The receptionists:
Laura, Amara, Jesse, Ashdig, Lorelai, Michael.
Bills will need to be paid. Trash cans emptied.

You'll want to kill the man at the market complaining
about his five-cent bottle deposit – you have to be friendly.
It's not their fault she won't eat anything you're buying.
Your main goal is to get something in her system besides
sodium chloride and carboplatin. You'll be relieved
every time she opens her eyes. She will become so frail
her pants practically fall off, she's too weak to bathe.
Sometimes, when she lies still, you can see her head
bobbing to her heartbeat. She will say one sentence,
it takes all her energy, one more word, and she's fast asleep.

The pamphlets never mention the sudden rage.
How you will want to stab everyone during breast cancer
awareness month. Everything is pink, even the MLB.
Would you like to donate a dollar for breast cancer
research? Oh, because breast cancer is the only cancer
that matters? Why can't we donate a dollar to general cancer?
Why don't we make the whole damn year
cancer awareness year? There are enough colors
and cancers to fill any 12 month calendar.
January: Colon, dark blue. February: Lung, white.
March: Bone, yellow. April: Skin, black. May: Prostate, light blue
June: Esophagus, periwinkle. July: Brain, gray.
August: Lymphoma, lime green. September: Ovarian, teal.
October: Breast, pink. November: Testicular, purple.
December: Leukemia, orange. Actually, forget it.
There's more than on this list, more than months. Don't forget it.
Don't say it. Don't tell the lady at the checkout counter
who tells you about breast cancer awareness month
that she isn't doing shit by wearing pink.
Don't say your grandmother had breast cancer and isn't wearing
pink. Don't say your grandmother is not wearing a pink bra.
One cup filled with pink silicon where her breast was chopped off.
That breast cancer exists every single month
whether or not it's breast cancer awareness month, whether or not

anybody wears pink – it's not only these four weeks, everybody is aware.
You're not doing a damn thing wearing pink and standing there.

FYI, medical marijuana is only frowned upon until asked for.
You've never touched the stuff yourself but it works, heck, it cures.
People are embarrassed to talk about it, though it's legal.
Even the Dean of Admissions at school will tell you it helped her son.
A nurse will whisper to you, *medical marijuana, amazing stuff* as though
she's selling it herself out of the kangaroo pouch in her scrubs.
Her doctor will say, *that's a spectacular idea, I fully support it!*
Although he never suggested it. She will bring home lollipop weed,
brownie weed,
a small electronic pipe, and weed pills to be refrigerated.
None of which will get her high at all, but will make her, ironically, stop
feeling green. After five cycles, it'll be the only thing
that stops her from feeling nauseous and vomiting. She tells everyone
how it helped her, and when we pass the store, she points and beams,
That's where your Mamma gets her weed!

The pamphlets don't mention the hospital bills
will be incorrect, overcharged. That your doctor who was
on your plan is no longer on your plan.
That we're not talking two hundred dollars –
we're talking $23,483 and 86 cents. Don't forget
the 86 cents. Your insurance covered 356 dollars
and 86 cents. When she can't stop throwing up,
when she's nauseous after three days,
you'll be on hold with Blue Cross for an hour
47 minutes and counting. *Your call is important
to us. Please wait, someone will be with you
shortly.* As if waiting is a choice, as if the person
who billed this as an "optional procedure"
knew anyone who had "optional cancer".
As if there's a month, color, and ribbon for that.
It was "optional" to get it removed. She was like maybe
I should get the surgery or die,

tough decision, maybe flip a coin, choose.
It was obviously elective. Don't worry. They'll be
with you shortly. Please wait. Your call is important.

In the waiting room, when she's throwing up
again, a man will come over and ask, *Is she
okay?* And you must hold back the urge to ask,
Are you completely fucking stupid? And
instead say, *She's nauseous
today. We've been waiting 30 minutes to get in.*
And he will look frantic, even accidentally run into
the wall, before finding someone to assist you.
You will not be ashamed of the glances shot your way,
in fact, you want to stand on a chair and say, *People of the
cancer center, this is what you have to look
forward to.* You'll want to create a pamphlet entitled:

Welcome to Hell, Friends!:
Here's what you should really know about cancer,
they will never tell you, but you deserve to know
the truth.

Keith Quarters

In Memory of Keith Abate

There are two men at my door,
black uniforms and gold medallions—
if I don't open it
maybe they'll be on their way.

If I don't open it
it will not happen:
his twin brother
an American flag
a 21-gun salute
pall-bearers.

There are two men at my door
if I keep it closed long enough
maybe he'll be knocking
smoking a La Flor Dominicana
celebrating being home again.

If I don't open it
his dog Layla won't be waiting,
the leather Jets jacket hanging,
no unsmoked cigars in a wooden box.
His mother, five nieces, and four nephews.

I collect Keith quarters in your honor
in a pill case, in my glove box, everywhere I go,
thinking I'll give them to you soon.

They're on their way,
they'll be on their way.

I lock, block the peephole,

keep my eyes closed, anything
not to open that door.

The Pacific Design Center

A man fell
to his death. "Likely
suicide," they said, as if
he tripped, dropped off
eleven floors by accident or
saw his widow place her
hands over her ears to block
out the possibility of "on purpose."
130 showrooms –
furniture, decorating materials –
top interior design.
Post-Oscar parties,
multi-million dollar fundraisers,
a branch of MOCA,
two restaurants by Wolfgang Puck:
all inside, please come inside,
where it's likely suicide.

Outside, the building gleams waves
of sapphires in the sunlight,
an ocean without depth surrounded
by fishy businessmen and the L.A. rush,
bosses expecting more than nine to five,
suits on cells being asked
to reach nothing less than great heights
they likely will fall from.

Toast

My grandma is an unusual case
though she sits across the table like an ordinary
woman. And laughs with her hands
over her mouth like a girl. I know under her blouse
there is one pad for a breast, chunks of her skin
missing, along with her ovaries.

I see what it takes
for her to get dressed in the morning
and pretend nothing's missing.
How when she's tired it's not because
she's 90. It's, "this body,
what this body has endured
is exhausting." She asks if I can take her
to an appointment tomorrow.
We're already going to one today. Over toast and eggs,

I look at her and say, "Actually,
I'm busy. I'm going to Paris. I can't take you."
She lights up like the Eiffel Tower at midnight
and cues her music box giggle. "Paris, huh?
What a character I got for a grandchild. Where did we get you?"
I reach for her left hand, tracing a crevice by her thumb,
"I love you," I say, and she says it back, holding on.

Concrete

"That's enough."
Lowering my gaze
in case
she didn't.
With every ounce of blood pumping
my veins that relayed to my fists
now tightly wound,
ready to sail.
Then softer, ashamed of her
still trying to speak.
"That's enough."

The group of black girls,
high school freshmen maybe,
playing at a bus stop in Providence
the way high school girls do,
girls who laugh and push
who say, "oh, I knew you liked him!"
Girls like any girls of any color.

Amy was from New Hampshire,
a suburb of whites, limped
with that crutch,
was on the ground when I told her
get up,
don't use those props around me,
understood her act perfectly,
wasn't putting up with that shit.

Ashlee looked at me
Ashlee, snow white, from the suburbs
sought culture. Ashlee with an open mind
to match her determined heart.
Ashlee who soaked her freckles in tears.

Amy spat,
"ignorant black people"
causing me to turn into a wrecking ball,
arms wide, a machine aimed to destroy
every perfect tooth, my knuckles readied to teach
her tongue to retreat until it had
something substantial to say.

My face, now so close to hers
our foreheads touched,
in case she got smart with me,
my forehead a more viable option
than my fists.

"That's enough."
Then softer, "that's enough."
Enunciated every word,
every bit of saliva,
so Amy wouldn't miss
a syllable. "The only ignorant person here
is you."

I got on that bus
with those girls and Ashlee
leaving Amy to soak in
the orange burst of sun set.
Her white skin scorched
as the bus turned – I assume,
I don't know, didn't look back.

10B

Waiting for the doors to open
on the tenth floor, a woman,
gray hair, arms full of cardboard
boxes stares at me, at my laundry,
says *that's a nice sturdy bag,*
where'd you get that? I say, *this?*
Target. She says, *Target*
always has such marvelous things.
We get into the elevator, she
with her boxes, me with my laundry,
she stares at me again, sadly, opens
her mouth, sighs, *this is the first time*
I've been home since my husband died.
He died eight months ago. I inhale, gasp,
say *oh, I'm so sorry.* She says,
we were together eight years after
both our spouses passed. He was my
second husband. You don't get
second chances like that.
I nod. I don't have a boyfriend. I'm turning
25 on Sunday. I say, *that's lovely.*
She sighs, *my granddaughter is eight,*
my granddaughter asked me if I'd get
married again. I don't think I will.
The elevator doors open and I don't
want to go, leave her alone,
I want to give her a hug, tell her
I appreciate her for trusting me with her
story. For giving me more in nine flights
than some people have given me in nine years.
I shuffle my bag out with me, awkwardly,
I say, *If you need anything I'm in 10K.*
She says, *10B.* And somehow I manage to turn

and say, *Thank you*
as the doors between us slide shut.

Affliction

I hear I have OCD, ADD,
a pinch of gangrene.
I got a little cancer, diabetes in my genes,
doc in lab coat thinks I'm a lab rat
that's why he asks, never listens.
Last week he said my whole family history
is in remission. I maybe have some autism,
might require a slight incision,
memory loss, synapses that fire
alarmingly. Should see a chiropractor
for what I carry on my back,
and that mole on my collarbone? Paid a derm $50
for a five minute look at that. A bunch of money-grabbing,
over analyzing, hypochondriacs. *Don't run in concrete, stay away*
from train tracks. Don't eat gluten, carbs, anything
with wheat. Don't consume pork, chicken, any kind of meat.
Try Atkins. Better yet, try South Beach.
When in doubt, simplify your diet
and simply not eat. Thank you for waiting, your call is important,
we're here to help! Our number one priority: your overall health!
We'd love to explain your benefits, ma'am,
we just don't understand them ourselves!
My insurance covers eyes and ears, not heart attacks.
If you go outside, wear a mask, might contract swine or bird or gnats in
your urinary tract. It's in the fine print.
Did you read the fine print? 200 pages. Sign. Print.
Here's a copy to take with
your vitamin C, D6, turmeric pill,
take a fish oil supplement, not too much
or you'll start to form gills. Let me see
inside your ears.
Flash a light into your eyes.
Cough twice for me.
Say "ah" open up wide.

You have viral meningitis.
Chrohns. Maybe colitis.
To determine, we need an x-ray
of your lungs, brain, and butt.
You probably have a mild case of acid reflux.
Can you feel this?
Feel that?
Let me check your pulse.
Breathe in, breathe out,
deep one, now cough.
With this air quality,
best to not breathe at all.
Hide inside an anti-bac, silicon ball.
Build up lemon scented walls.
Be careful.
More careful.
Be extra cautious.
So prepared, I'm on the phone,
already calling in hospice.

I Am Erica

When I walk thru skid row
look at dust covered eyes
swear I've seen them before
writhing in cold,
under tattered sheets
I want to say *I am Erica*
we're here together
I'm not
I don't
I watch
women in red soled heels on 5th Ave
talking five pounds
comparing tags in handbags
I am Erica face painting stripes
and stars on the Fourth of July
celebrating those overseas
lighting up skies
I am home
of the brave
visiting graves
eating corn beets lettuce
passing dairy farms, wheat
in rows feeding off 50
different types of loaves
picking cola cans growing
in peppered sand
ground we covered
in flight
over city lights
into more siren sounds
when we touch down
same air in our lungs
as where we departed from
I am Erica wherever I go,

I am Erica, recall justice for all.
I, America, see you
fall.
Can't sleep
in headlights,
walk past cracked neon signs,
drink muddy coffee,
am asked for pennies,
by streaked reflections of me.

Such A Lovely Place (Such A Lovely Place)

That song always
comes on, to and from.
My mom, often weak,
sometimes sings
with her eyes
closed. Her lips
move with passing
brown and green palm
trees. Sometimes, when
strong, she nods her head,
taps her right thumb to
the bass drum.
Some dance to remember, some dance to forget.
Left on Doheny,
right on Beverly,
could draw the blueprint
of this building from memory.
Receptionist asks: last name?
Birthdate? Allergies?
Please, take a seat.
Plenty of room at The Hotel California.
Last night, Mom chucked
the only pound she'd gained.
I rubbed her back, gave her
a pill for nausea, a pill for pain.
In the waiting room, she donated
another meal, again. After four
hours of pills and IVs, she's
stumbling out the door, drunk on
sodium chloride and adavan, holding
onto me. I help her in, get in
the driver's seat. Car whirls
on, Mom falls asleep. Radio sings,
You can check-out any time you like, but you can never leave.

How to Be a Young Woman

Michela and I sit cross-legged,
fourteen, looking,
not appearing like women in *Vogue*
our curves too 3D for glossy pages.

Figuring shrinking would be easy,
not eating or drinking –
Michela and I, both shapely girls,
decide to be anorexic together,

gossip about boys we like,
chat to classmates online,
call Josh on speakerphone asking who he wanted,
giggle as he stutters through a response.

Talk about high school,
wonder what team we'll make for soccer,
gab excitedly about the *Sisterhood* book,
then, of course, gossip about boys again.

We lean back on our palms, absorbing
our conversation in silence
Michela breaks it, saying, "want to get a sandwich?"
So we go three blocks to The Farms and eat the works,
tossing *Vogue* into an alley trashcan on our way.

Cage

My rib cage is actually a birdcage
I let one lovely white dove fly
into the center core by your heart.
Sometimes I revel in sending it your way,
perhaps you needed more than I did.
Anyways this cage was getting heavy
from the wings flapping,
all the chirps I held inside
and couldn't let go. Today, walking around alone
in darkness where there should be street lights,
I've been thinking that I want my dove back.
After all, it was mine to give –
it should be mine to take back too.

I want to know flight
with or without it,
I want to feel fluttering again.

Heavy Lifting

At six I watched suitcases packed
with striped ties, brown loafers, suits.
Stood in my parents' walk-in closet
wondering how to fill empty
shelves. I found a red toolkit,
when nails came undone
I'd hammer them back into their holes.
When mom's handbag was out of reach
I'd climb a silver ladder. When my sister
couldn't hoist the Kitchen Aid mixer,
I'd lift it. When kids started rumors
about her, I'd crush them like spiders
I killed in bedroom corners. Cleared away
like cobwebs that gathered up.
Like hair that clogged our drains
I snaked out. Like toilets that wouldn't flush
until I replaced the chain.

When

She asked, "Can't we ride a bus anymore?"
No, we cannot speak in our tongue or they'll carve it out
of our disgusting Hebrew speaking mouths. Before
we could go to Paris, now, we can't even go to work
in the ruins of what we built with our bare blood. We can't
wear two triangles in certain formations, don't tell
a soul about our David, who we once thought
slayed Goliath, but clearly, has been reincarnated
into beards and brainwaves programmed to spill
our dirty guts down a 710 #40 Tel Aviv bus.
I say, "let's lock the doors, stand by the glimmer of light
slipping thru the window that must be shining down from
our God." Where's our sun gone? Our festival? Now it's
miraculous if there's eight days without one of us six feet under.
Now they're not settling only for our first-born.
Goliath won't be quenched until he drains all of our kin.
Our mere soles hitting concrete is a sin. We are cockroaches
infesting their walls, they came to fumigate. We are the polyp
in their throats, not clearing away. We are in our homeland looking
over our yellow starred shoulders. Hiding dangerous symbols
we can't wear like medallions anymore. Possess a pendant
they'll park shells in your ribs like they did your relatives
by the thousands. We can't breathe their air. We're taking
nature's elements that belong to them. I can't imagine their God
resides in heaven. She asked, "What will we do when they come for us?"
And I said, "What do you mean 'when'?"

Exhibition Game

We do not stare at the empty chair.
When it glances at us, we avoid eye contact.
Grams scolds Gramps for eating too much salt.
Gramps eats more than he talks.
There is only clinking silverware
and silence so sharp it rivals a shattered
windshield. We ask each other to pass
dishes only to transport time.
My sister and I push mashed potatoes around
our plates. We were not born when the chair
was filled. We have learned from picture frames
and my middle name. The long dining room table
is never at capacity. Could fit another family.
Once heard Gram's door slam, say she wished that empty
seat was mommy. Some nights, after dessert,
Gramps would vanish to the "bathroom." I'd follow him
down the hall to his room where he watched the Lakers
in his leather La-Z-Boy. I'd sit at his feet by the screen.
Even when they were down 20 at the half he'd say, "Kobe!"
He'd say, "Gotta believe" and "You better believe it!"
Sometimes we'd merely witness miracles.
When the game was over, he'd turn off the TV,
help me up, and as we headed towards the hall,
setting out for the dining room table,
he'd pat me on the head and say,
"Showtime, kiddo."

Being Human

My father growled at an employee
at Carl's Jr. by CSUN.
He said, "We need our chicken sandwiches now!
We are going to a funeral.
We need to hurry."
My father hardly ever yells.

In the foyer, we stared at Mack's photo
waiting for him to talk,
like in cartoons he'd escape the frame,
come to life, say,
"What you staring at, Weiss?"

And Gail in her black widow dress
did a fantastic job pretending she was,
"Fine, really, just fine" but we could see
she was protesting sleep
since now it meant alone.

Inside, I put my hand on my father's shoulder
and he nodded
business-like
Gail stood at the front
gravely
said, "Let's celebrate my husband's life."

My father, amidst candlelight,
told stories of long rides together,
long talks with each other,
Mack always saying,
"What you think about that, Weiss?"

My father, dripping like wax for Mack
unable to celebrate his life without him.
Cannot say to me and my sister

"My buddy Mack" anymore without
"gone". My father hardly ever cries.

When he did, it was the first time
I realized my father is human.
That Mack was human and Gail too.

When Gail vanished for months
leaving only the answering machine,
"Mack and Gail aren't here right now…"
It was the first time I saw my father cry.

I walked out of the service, sick
of aneurysms, heart attacks,
and lymphoma. Sick
of commemorative photos
and telling folks what they mean to me
too late for them to listen.

But mostly, I am so damn sick
of everyone I know
being human.

Malignant Neoplasm

My grandmother is brave in the dressing room
lifting her sweater, revealing a medical tag,
slipping the blue gown on, slit open to front, holding it closed,
all in one motion – so robotic
it's sickening, forced into this routine –
her second home is this hospital wing.

Her appointment book is filled
with more doctors than friends.
At radiation, she answers her birthdate with
"I'm older than this goddamn place"
and we laugh to destroy the pain.

Outside, a nurse approaches me:
I'm sorry, miss, but you can't be here.
I'm family.
The radiation might get you if you're too close.

Then why are you here?
Did you go to an alternate universe at nursing school

allowing immunity?
Maybe it will serve as an antibiotic.
Does it affect your ears too?
Perhaps you didn't hear:
I'm. Not. Moving.

The government gives my grandmother six free bras a year –
that's nice, but no consolation prize for being a body
between a whirling machine that takes our faith.
Machine, if you're working, why
has my grandma had a "malignant neoplasm" three times?

Sometimes I call her though I have nothing to say.
When she answers, I let my breath go.

One day my aunt has it in her cervix.
How did it get there? *We're working on it.*

My aunt caresses my hair while sitting on the couch.
Mine is waist length. Hers is gone.
She thinks I'm wonderful.
She buys scarves and smiles so hard –
sometimes almost convincing me she's okay.

When I knock vases, break glasses she tells me to grin.
I don't understand how she can stay positive –
it feels good to smash things.

There's a girl in the hospital – she's probably three or four –
has a scar on her brain where her crown should be.
She carries an IV behind her where dolls should swing.
I tell her she's beautiful and she smiles.

Sometimes, I lose it, seeing my grandmother in the dressing room.
Before the hospital, we order garden scrambles and passion tea –
she's telling jokes, laughing, and she's
here. Like my aunt whose hair is growing back.

I look for that girl in the hospital every time we go,
I never see her again.

Cannibals

We are so delicate in our shells
Should all read *handle with care*
We are being pried open in commotion
Forgetting our hands can crush

We say *how are you*
Respond, *vanilla latte no foam*
We say *tell me about it*
Put on headphones
We say *I feel you*
Without fingertips or arms
We say *technology is ruining us*
Read e-mails at dinner tables
We say hold the door
Can't carry a conversation
We start sentences with *I*
Never looking into irises

We say *life is hard*
We say *it'll get easier*
We say *keep going*
We say *when does it end*
We say *give love*
We say *take care*

We are each one egg of a dozen
Not checking if any are broken
Cracking them open
Only when we're hungry

About the Author

Julia Gari Weiss received her MFA from Sarah Lawrence College. She is the recipient of the Academy of American Poet's John B. Santoianni Award for Excellence in Poetry. Julia has been published in *3Elements Review, Image Curve, The Australian Women's Weekly, Thought Catalog, Old Red Kimono,* and *The Santa Monica Star.* She currently lives in Brooklyn, New York.

Thought Catalog, it's a website.

www.thoughtcatalog.com

Social

facebook.com/thoughtcatalog
twitter.com/thoughtcatalog
tumblr.com/thoughtcatalog
instagram.com/thoughtcatalog

Corporate

www.thought.is

Made in the USA
Columbia, SC
01 February 2018